# 50 30-Minute Weeknight Recipes for Home

By: Kelly Johnson

# Table of Contents

- Grilled Cedar Plank Salmon
- Dutch Oven Beef Bourguignon
- Campfire Paella
- Foil Packet Garlic Butter Shrimp
- Cast Iron Skillet Cornbread
- Stuffed Bell Peppers with Quinoa and Black Beans
- Campfire Pizza with Fresh Mozzarella and Basil
- Sweet Potato and Black Bean Chili
- Campfire Jambalaya
- Grilled Vegetable Skewers with Balsamic Glaze
- Campfire Apple Crisp
- Campfire French Toast
- Moroccan Spiced Lamb Kebabs
- Coconut Curry Lentil Soup
- Campfire Brie with Honey and Almonds
- Grilled Portobello Mushroom Burgers
- Campfire Tacos with Homemade Guacamole
- Foil Packet Lemon Herb Chicken
- Dutch Oven Lasagna
- Campfire Banana S'mores
- Cajun Shrimp Foil Packets
- Skillet Sausage and Potato Hash
- Campfire Garlic Butter Lobster Tails
- Campfire Quesadillas with Caramelized Onions
- Dutch Oven Chicken Cacciatore
- Campfire Ratatouille
- Foil Packet Teriyaki Salmon
- Grilled Peach and Burrata Salad
- Campfire Stuffed Peppers with Sausage and Rice
- Dutch Oven Lemon Herb Roast Chicken
- Campfire Nachos with Homemade Pico de Gallo
- Foil Packet BBQ Ribs
- Campfire Vegetable Curry
- Skillet Garlic Butter Steak
- Dutch Oven Vegetable Soup
- Campfire Macaroni and Cheese

- Foil Packet Mediterranean Salmon
- Campfire Pesto Pasta with Cherry Tomatoes
- Dutch Oven Chicken and Dumplings
- Campfire Ratatouille Stuffed Mushrooms
- Grilled Halloumi and Vegetable Skewers
- Foil Packet Honey Garlic Chicken
- Campfire Stuffed Apples with Cinnamon
- Dutch Oven Beef Stew
- Campfire Breakfast Burritos
- Foil Packet Lemon Herb Tilapia
- Skillet Chicken Alfredo
- Campfire Caprese Salad
- Dutch Oven Vegetarian Chili
- Campfire Sausage and Potato Foil Packets

**Grilled Cedar Plank Salmon**

Ingredients:

- 1 cedar plank (soaked in water for at least 1 hour)
- 4 salmon fillets (6 ounces each), skin on
- Salt and pepper, to taste
- 2 tablespoons olive oil
- 2 tablespoons honey
- 2 tablespoons Dijon mustard
- 2 tablespoons soy sauce
- 2 cloves garlic, minced
- Fresh lemon wedges, for serving
- Fresh dill, for garnish (optional)

Instructions:

1. Preheat your grill to medium-high heat (about 375-400°F or 190-200°C).
2. In a small bowl, whisk together the olive oil, honey, Dijon mustard, soy sauce, and minced garlic to make the marinade.
3. Pat the salmon fillets dry with paper towels and season them with salt and pepper on both sides.
4. Place the soaked cedar plank on the grill and close the lid. Let it heat up for about 3-5 minutes until it begins to smoke and char slightly.
5. Place the seasoned salmon fillets skin-side down on the cedar plank, arranging them evenly with some space between each fillet.
6. Brush the marinade generously over the top of each salmon fillet, coating them evenly.
7. Close the grill lid and cook the salmon for about 12-15 minutes, or until it flakes easily with a fork and reaches an internal temperature of 145°F (63°C).
8. Carefully remove the cedar plank with the cooked salmon from the grill using heatproof gloves or tongs.
9. Serve the grilled cedar plank salmon immediately with fresh lemon wedges on the side for squeezing over the top. Garnish with fresh dill, if desired.

Enjoy your delicious Grilled Cedar Plank Salmon straight from the campfire!

**Dutch Oven Beef Bourguignon**

Ingredients:

- 2 pounds (about 900g) beef chuck roast, cut into 1-inch cubes
- Salt and black pepper, to taste
- 2 tablespoons olive oil
- 4 slices bacon, chopped
- 1 onion, diced
- 3 cloves garlic, minced
- 2 carrots, peeled and sliced
- 2 stalks celery, sliced
- 8 ounces (about 225g) mushrooms, sliced
- 2 tablespoons all-purpose flour
- 2 cups (480ml) beef broth
- 1 cup (240ml) red wine (such as Burgundy or Pinot Noir)
- 2 tablespoons tomato paste
- 2 bay leaves
- 1 teaspoon dried thyme
- 1 teaspoon dried rosemary
- 1 tablespoon Worcestershire sauce
- Chopped fresh parsley, for garnish

Instructions:

1. Season the beef cubes with salt and black pepper to taste.
2. Heat the olive oil in a Dutch oven over medium-high heat. Add the seasoned beef cubes and cook until browned on all sides, about 5-7 minutes. Remove the beef from the Dutch oven and set aside.
3. In the same Dutch oven, add the chopped bacon and cook until crispy. Remove the bacon with a slotted spoon and set aside, leaving the bacon drippings in the pot.
4. Add the diced onion to the Dutch oven and cook until softened, about 3-4 minutes. Add the minced garlic and cook for an additional 1 minute.
5. Add the sliced carrots, celery, and mushrooms to the Dutch oven. Cook, stirring occasionally, until the vegetables are slightly softened, about 5 minutes.
6. Sprinkle the flour over the vegetables and stir to coat. Cook for 1-2 minutes to remove the raw flour taste.
7. Gradually pour in the beef broth and red wine, stirring constantly to avoid lumps. Add the tomato paste, bay leaves, dried thyme, dried rosemary, and Worcestershire sauce. Stir to combine.
8. Return the browned beef cubes and crispy bacon to the Dutch oven. Stir everything together.

9. Cover the Dutch oven with a lid and place it over low heat, allowing the beef bourguignon to simmer gently for 2-3 hours, or until the beef is tender and the flavors have melded together. Stir occasionally and adjust the heat as needed to maintain a gentle simmer.
10. Once the beef bourguignon is ready, taste and adjust the seasoning with salt and pepper if necessary. Remove the bay leaves before serving.
11. Garnish the Dutch Oven Beef Bourguignon with chopped fresh parsley and serve hot, preferably with crusty bread or mashed potatoes to soak up the flavorful sauce.

Enjoy your comforting Dutch Oven Beef Bourguignon cooked over the campfire!

**Campfire Paella**

Ingredients:

- 1 pound (about 450g) chicken thighs, boneless and skinless, cut into bite-sized pieces
- 1 pound (about 450g) Spanish chorizo, sliced
- 1 onion, finely chopped
- 3 cloves garlic, minced
- 1 red bell pepper, diced
- 1 yellow bell pepper, diced
- 1 cup (200g) cherry tomatoes, halved
- 1 cup (200g) frozen peas
- 2 cups (400g) Spanish paella rice (bomba rice or arborio rice can be substituted)
- 4 cups (960ml) chicken broth
- 1 teaspoon smoked paprika
- 1 teaspoon saffron threads (optional)
- Salt and black pepper, to taste
- Olive oil, for cooking
- Lemon wedges, for serving
- Fresh parsley, chopped, for garnish

Instructions:

1. Set up your campfire or grill with a sturdy cooking grate. Place a large paella pan or skillet over the flame to preheat.
2. Drizzle some olive oil into the preheated pan. Add the chicken pieces and chorizo slices. Cook, stirring occasionally, until the chicken is browned and cooked through, and the chorizo is slightly crispy. Remove the chicken and chorizo from the pan and set aside.
3. In the same pan, add a bit more olive oil if needed. Add the chopped onion and cook until softened, about 3-4 minutes. Add the minced garlic and cook for another minute until fragrant.
4. Stir in the diced bell peppers and cherry tomatoes. Cook for a few minutes until the vegetables are slightly softened.
5. Add the paella rice to the pan, stirring to coat it in the oil and vegetables. Cook for 1-2 minutes to lightly toast the rice.
6. Pour the chicken broth into the pan, along with the smoked paprika and saffron threads, if using. Season with salt and black pepper to taste. Stir everything together.
7. Return the cooked chicken and chorizo to the pan, spreading them out evenly over the rice mixture.
8. Cover the pan with a lid or aluminum foil and let the paella cook over the campfire for about 20-25 minutes, or until the rice is tender and has absorbed most of the liquid. Avoid stirring too much to develop the coveted crispy layer of rice, known as socarrat, on the bottom.

9. During the last 5 minutes of cooking, scatter the frozen peas over the paella and continue cooking until they're heated through.
10. Once the paella is cooked, remove it from the heat and let it rest for a few minutes. Garnish with freshly chopped parsley and serve hot with lemon wedges on the side.

Enjoy your flavorful Campfire Paella, perfect for sharing with friends and family outdoors!

**Foil Packet Garlic Butter Shrimp**

Ingredients:

- 1 pound (about 450g) large shrimp, peeled and deveined
- 4 tablespoons unsalted butter, melted
- 4 cloves garlic, minced
- 2 tablespoons fresh parsley, chopped
- 1 tablespoon lemon juice
- Salt and black pepper, to taste
- Lemon wedges, for serving
- Chopped fresh parsley, for garnish
- Heavy-duty aluminum foil

Instructions:

1. Preheat your campfire or grill to medium-high heat.
2. In a small bowl, combine the melted butter, minced garlic, chopped parsley, lemon juice, salt, and black pepper. Stir until well combined.
3. Tear off four pieces of heavy-duty aluminum foil, each about 12 inches long.
4. Divide the peeled and deveined shrimp evenly among the foil packets, placing them in the center of each foil sheet.
5. Spoon the garlic butter mixture evenly over the shrimp in each packet, ensuring that the shrimp are well coated.
6. Fold the sides of each foil packet over the shrimp to form a sealed pouch, leaving a little room for steam to circulate inside.
7. Place the foil packets directly onto the preheated grill grate or campfire coals. Cook for about 8-10 minutes, or until the shrimp are pink and opaque, and cooked through.
8. Carefully remove the foil packets from the heat using tongs or heatproof gloves.
9. Open the foil packets carefully to avoid burning yourself with the steam. Be cautious of the hot steam that will escape when opening.
10. Serve the Foil Packet Garlic Butter Shrimp hot, garnished with additional chopped parsley and lemon wedges on the side for squeezing over the shrimp.

Enjoy your succulent and flavorful Foil Packet Garlic Butter Shrimp straight from the campfire!

**Cast Iron Skillet Cornbread**

Ingredients:

- 1 cup (120g) cornmeal
- 1 cup (125g) all-purpose flour
- 1/4 cup (50g) granulated sugar
- 1 tablespoon baking powder
- 1/2 teaspoon salt
- 1 cup (240ml) buttermilk
- 1/2 cup (120ml) milk
- 2 large eggs
- 1/4 cup (60ml) unsalted butter, melted
- 2 tablespoons vegetable oil or bacon grease, for greasing the skillet

Instructions:

1. Preheat your campfire or grill to medium heat, or if using a campfire, prepare a bed of coals.
2. Place a 10-inch cast iron skillet on the campfire grate or directly on the coals to preheat. Add the vegetable oil or bacon grease to the skillet, spreading it evenly across the bottom and sides.
3. In a large mixing bowl, whisk together the cornmeal, all-purpose flour, sugar, baking powder, and salt until well combined.
4. In a separate bowl, whisk together the buttermilk, milk, eggs, and melted butter until smooth.
5. Pour the wet ingredients into the dry ingredients and stir until just combined. Be careful not to overmix; a few lumps are okay.
6. Carefully remove the preheated cast iron skillet from the campfire or grill using heatproof gloves or oven mitts.
7. Pour the cornbread batter into the hot skillet, spreading it out evenly with a spatula.
8. Place the skillet back onto the campfire grate or coals, cover with a lid if available, and cook for 20-25 minutes, or until the cornbread is golden brown on top and a toothpick inserted into the center comes out clean.
9. Once cooked, remove the skillet from the heat and let the cornbread cool slightly before slicing and serving.
10. Serve the Cast Iron Skillet Cornbread warm, either as a side dish or on its own. It's delicious with a drizzle of honey or served alongside chili, barbecue, or stew.

Enjoy your homemade Cast Iron Skillet Cornbread, made right over the campfire!

**Stuffed Bell Peppers with Quinoa and Black Beans**

Ingredients:

- 4 large bell peppers, any color
- 1 cup (180g) quinoa, rinsed
- 2 cups (480ml) vegetable broth or water
- 1 tablespoon olive oil
- 1 onion, diced
- 2 cloves garlic, minced
- 1 can (15 ounces) black beans, drained and rinsed
- 1 can (14.5 ounces) diced tomatoes, drained
- 1 teaspoon ground cumin
- 1 teaspoon chili powder
- Salt and pepper, to taste
- 1 cup (120g) shredded cheese (cheddar, Monterey Jack, or Mexican blend)
- Chopped fresh cilantro or parsley, for garnish (optional)

Instructions:

1. Prepare your campfire or grill for medium heat, or if using a campfire, ensure you have a bed of hot coals.
2. Cut the tops off the bell peppers and remove the seeds and membranes. Set aside.
3. In a medium saucepan, combine the rinsed quinoa and vegetable broth or water. Bring to a boil, then reduce the heat to low, cover, and simmer for 15-20 minutes, or until the quinoa is cooked and the liquid is absorbed. Remove from heat and fluff with a fork.
4. While the quinoa is cooking, heat the olive oil in a large skillet over medium heat. Add the diced onion and cook until softened, about 5 minutes. Add the minced garlic and cook for an additional minute until fragrant.
5. Stir in the black beans, diced tomatoes, ground cumin, chili powder, cooked quinoa, salt, and pepper. Cook for another 2-3 minutes, allowing the flavors to meld together. Taste and adjust seasoning if needed.
6. Stuff each bell pepper with the quinoa and black bean mixture, pressing down gently to pack it in. Top each pepper with shredded cheese.

7. Place the stuffed bell peppers in a cast iron skillet or on a grilling tray, ensuring they're stable and won't tip over.
8. Transfer the skillet or tray to the campfire grate or grill. Cover with a lid or foil and cook for 20-25 minutes, or until the peppers are tender and the cheese is melted and bubbly.
9. Carefully remove the stuffed bell peppers from the heat using heatproof gloves or oven mitts.
10. Garnish the stuffed bell peppers with chopped fresh cilantro or parsley, if desired, before serving.

Enjoy your delicious Stuffed Bell Peppers with Quinoa and Black Beans, a satisfying and wholesome camping meal!

**Campfire Pizza with Fresh Mozzarella and Basil**

Ingredients:

- Pizza dough (store-bought or homemade)
- Olive oil, for brushing
- 1 cup (240ml) pizza sauce
- 8 ounces (about 225g) fresh mozzarella cheese, sliced
- Fresh basil leaves, torn
- Optional toppings: sliced tomatoes, sliced mushrooms, sliced bell peppers, olives, etc.

Instructions:

1. Prepare your campfire or grill for medium-high heat, ensuring you have a bed of hot coals or an even flame.
2. Roll out the pizza dough on a lightly floured surface to your desired thickness. You can divide the dough into smaller portions for individual-sized pizzas or keep it as one large pizza.
3. Brush one side of the rolled-out dough with olive oil.
4. Carefully transfer the oiled side of the dough onto a preheated cast iron skillet or a pizza stone placed over the campfire grate. Place it oiled-side down.
5. Cook the dough for 2-3 minutes, or until it starts to puff up and develop grill marks on the bottom. Use tongs or a spatula to flip the dough over.
6. Quickly spread pizza sauce over the cooked side of the dough, leaving a small border around the edges.
7. Arrange the sliced fresh mozzarella evenly over the sauce.
8. Add any additional toppings you desire, such as sliced tomatoes, mushrooms, bell peppers, or olives.
9. Cover the skillet with a lid or aluminum foil and let the pizza cook for another 5-7 minutes, or until the cheese is melted and bubbly, and the crust is golden brown.
10. Carefully remove the skillet from the campfire using heatproof gloves or oven mitts.
11. Sprinkle torn fresh basil leaves over the hot pizza.
12. Allow the pizza to cool for a minute or two before slicing and serving.

Enjoy your delicious Campfire Pizza with Fresh Mozzarella and Basil, a perfect fireside meal for camping adventures!

**Sweet Potato and Black Bean Chili**

Ingredients:

- 2 tablespoons olive oil
- 1 onion, diced
- 3 cloves garlic, minced
- 2 medium sweet potatoes, peeled and diced
- 1 red bell pepper, diced
- 1 green bell pepper, diced
- 1 jalapeño pepper, seeded and diced (optional, for added heat)
- 2 teaspoons ground cumin
- 1 teaspoon smoked paprika
- 1/2 teaspoon chili powder
- 1/2 teaspoon dried oregano
- 1 can (15 ounces) black beans, drained and rinsed
- 1 can (14.5 ounces) diced tomatoes, with juices
- 2 cups (480ml) vegetable broth
- Salt and black pepper, to taste
- Fresh cilantro, chopped, for garnish
- Avocado slices, for garnish (optional)
- Lime wedges, for serving

Instructions:

1. Heat the olive oil in a large Dutch oven or pot over medium heat, either on a campfire grate or a camp stove.
2. Add the diced onion and cook until softened, about 3-4 minutes.
3. Add the minced garlic and cook for another minute until fragrant.
4. Stir in the diced sweet potatoes, red bell pepper, green bell pepper, and jalapeño pepper (if using). Cook for 5-7 minutes, stirring occasionally, until the vegetables begin to soften.
5. Add the ground cumin, smoked paprika, chili powder, and dried oregano to the pot. Stir to coat the vegetables in the spices and cook for another minute to toast the spices.
6. Pour in the drained and rinsed black beans, diced tomatoes (with their juices), and vegetable broth. Stir everything together.
7. Bring the chili to a simmer and then reduce the heat to low. Cover the pot and let the chili cook for 20-25 minutes, or until the sweet potatoes are tender, stirring occasionally.
8. Once the sweet potatoes are cooked through, taste the chili and season with salt and black pepper as needed.
9. Ladle the Sweet Potato and Black Bean Chili into bowls and garnish with chopped fresh cilantro. If desired, serve with avocado slices and lime wedges on the side.

10. Enjoy your comforting and flavorful Sweet Potato and Black Bean Chili, perfect for warming up around the campfire!

**Campfire Jambalaya**

Ingredients:

- 1 tablespoon olive oil
- 1 onion, diced
- 1 bell pepper (any color), diced
- 2 celery stalks, diced
- 3 cloves garlic, minced
- 1 pound (about 450g) Andouille sausage, sliced
- 1 pound (about 450g) chicken breasts or thighs, diced
- 1 can (14.5 ounces) diced tomatoes, undrained
- 1 cup (200g) long-grain white rice
- 2 cups (480ml) chicken broth
- 1 teaspoon smoked paprika
- 1 teaspoon dried thyme
- 1 teaspoon dried oregano
- 1/2 teaspoon cayenne pepper (adjust to taste)
- Salt and black pepper, to taste
- 1 pound (about 450g) large shrimp, peeled and deveined
- Chopped fresh parsley, for garnish

Instructions:

1. Heat the olive oil in a large Dutch oven or pot over medium heat, either on a campfire grate or a camp stove.
2. Add the diced onion, bell pepper, and celery to the pot. Cook, stirring occasionally, until the vegetables are softened, about 5-7 minutes.
3. Add the minced garlic to the pot and cook for another minute until fragrant.
4. Stir in the sliced Andouille sausage and diced chicken. Cook until the chicken is browned on all sides, about 5-7 minutes.
5. Add the diced tomatoes (undrained), rice, chicken broth, smoked paprika, dried thyme, dried oregano, and cayenne pepper to the pot. Season with salt and black pepper to taste.
6. Stir everything together, ensuring the rice is submerged in the liquid. Bring the mixture to a simmer.
7. Once simmering, cover the pot and let the Jambalaya cook for 20-25 minutes, or until the rice is tender and the liquid is absorbed, stirring occasionally to prevent sticking.
8. When the rice is almost done, add the peeled and deveined shrimp to the pot. Cook for an additional 3-5 minutes, or until the shrimp are pink and cooked through.
9. Once everything is cooked through, taste the Jambalaya and adjust the seasoning if needed.
10. Garnish the Campfire Jambalaya with chopped fresh parsley before serving.

11. Enjoy your flavorful and comforting Campfire Jambalaya, perfect for sharing around the fire with friends and family!

**Grilled Vegetable Skewers with Balsamic Glaze**

Ingredients:

- Assorted vegetables, such as bell peppers, zucchini, cherry tomatoes, mushrooms, red onions, and yellow squash, cut into bite-sized pieces
- Wooden or metal skewers
- Olive oil, for brushing
- Salt and black pepper, to taste
- Balsamic Glaze (you can use store-bought or make your own):
    - 1/2 cup (120ml) balsamic vinegar
    - 2 tablespoons honey or maple syrup (optional, for sweetness)

Instructions:

1. If using wooden skewers, soak them in water for at least 30 minutes before grilling to prevent them from burning.
2. Preheat your grill or campfire to medium-high heat.
3. Thread the assorted vegetable pieces onto the skewers, alternating colors and varieties for an attractive presentation.
4. Brush the vegetable skewers with olive oil and season with salt and black pepper to taste.
5. Place the skewers on the preheated grill or campfire grate. Cook for 8-10 minutes, turning occasionally, until the vegetables are tender and slightly charred.
6. While the vegetable skewers are grilling, prepare the balsamic glaze. In a small saucepan, combine the balsamic vinegar and honey or maple syrup (if using) over medium heat. Bring the mixture to a simmer and cook for 8-10 minutes, or until it has reduced by half and thickened to a glaze-like consistency. Remove from heat and set aside.
7. Once the vegetable skewers are cooked, transfer them to a serving platter.
8. Drizzle the grilled vegetable skewers with the balsamic glaze just before serving, or serve the glaze on the side for dipping.
9. Enjoy your delicious Grilled Vegetable Skewers with Balsamic Glaze as a flavorful and colorful side dish or appetizer at your next outdoor gathering!

Feel free to adjust the vegetable selection based on your preferences and what's in season. These skewers are versatile and can be customized to suit your tastes!

**Campfire Apple Crisp**

Ingredients:

- 6-8 medium apples, peeled, cored, and thinly sliced
- 1 tablespoon lemon juice
- 1/2 cup (100g) granulated sugar
- 1 teaspoon ground cinnamon
- 1/4 teaspoon ground nutmeg
- 1 cup (100g) old-fashioned rolled oats
- 1/2 cup (100g) all-purpose flour
- 1/2 cup (100g) packed brown sugar
- 1/2 cup (115g) unsalted butter, cold and cut into small cubes
- Pinch of salt
- Vanilla ice cream or whipped cream, for serving (optional)

Instructions:

1. Prepare your campfire or grill for medium heat, ensuring you have a bed of hot coals or an even flame.
2. In a large bowl, toss the sliced apples with lemon juice to prevent browning.
3. In a small bowl, mix together the granulated sugar, ground cinnamon, and ground nutmeg.
4. Sprinkle the sugar and spice mixture over the sliced apples, tossing to coat evenly. Set aside.
5. In another bowl, combine the rolled oats, all-purpose flour, packed brown sugar, and a pinch of salt.
6. Add the cold cubed butter to the oat mixture. Using your fingertips or a pastry cutter, work the butter into the dry ingredients until the mixture resembles coarse crumbs. It's okay if there are some larger chunks of butter.
7. Evenly spread the seasoned apple slices in the bottom of a cast iron skillet or Dutch oven.
8. Sprinkle the oat topping evenly over the apples, covering them completely.
9. Cover the skillet or Dutch oven with aluminum foil, ensuring it's tightly sealed around the edges.
10. Place the covered skillet or Dutch oven on the campfire grate or directly onto the hot coals. Cook for about 30-40 minutes, or until the apples are tender and bubbling, and the topping is golden brown and crisp. Check occasionally to ensure the crisp doesn't burn, adjusting the heat as needed.
11. Once the Campfire Apple Crisp is cooked through, carefully remove it from the heat using heatproof gloves or oven mitts.
12. Allow the crisp to cool slightly before serving. Serve warm, topped with vanilla ice cream or whipped cream if desired.

Enjoy your delicious and comforting Campfire Apple Crisp, perfect for enjoying under the stars!

**Campfire French Toast**

Ingredients:

- 8 slices of bread (day-old bread works best)
- 4 eggs
- 1/2 cup (120ml) milk
- 1 teaspoon vanilla extract
- 1/2 teaspoon ground cinnamon
- Pinch of salt
- Butter or cooking oil, for greasing the skillet
- Maple syrup, for serving
- Optional toppings: fresh berries, sliced bananas, powdered sugar, whipped cream, etc.

Instructions:

1. Preheat your campfire or grill to medium heat, ensuring you have a bed of hot coals or an even flame.
2. In a shallow dish or bowl, whisk together the eggs, milk, vanilla extract, ground cinnamon, and a pinch of salt until well combined.
3. Dip each slice of bread into the egg mixture, allowing it to soak for a few seconds on each side.
4. Heat a cast iron skillet or griddle over the campfire grate or directly on the hot coals. Grease the skillet with butter or cooking oil.
5. Place the soaked bread slices onto the hot skillet. Cook for 2-3 minutes on each side, or until golden brown and cooked through.
6. Repeat with the remaining bread slices, adding more butter or oil to the skillet as needed.
7. Once all the French toast slices are cooked, remove them from the skillet and transfer them to serving plates.
8. Serve the Campfire French Toast warm, drizzled with maple syrup and topped with your choice of optional toppings, such as fresh berries, sliced bananas, powdered sugar, or whipped cream.
9. Enjoy your delicious Campfire French Toast as a satisfying and hearty breakfast to fuel your outdoor adventures!

Feel free to customize the French toast by using different types of bread or adding your favorite spices or flavorings to the egg mixture. It's a versatile recipe that can be adapted to suit your preferences!

**Moroccan Spiced Lamb Kebabs**

Ingredients:

- 1.5 pounds (about 680g) lamb leg or shoulder, cut into 1-inch cubes
- 1 onion, finely chopped
- 3 cloves garlic, minced
- 2 tablespoons fresh cilantro, chopped
- 2 tablespoons fresh parsley, chopped
- 1 tablespoon ground cumin
- 1 tablespoon ground coriander
- 1 teaspoon ground cinnamon
- 1 teaspoon ground paprika
- 1/2 teaspoon ground turmeric
- 1/2 teaspoon ground ginger
- 1/4 teaspoon cayenne pepper (adjust to taste)
- Salt and black pepper, to taste
- 2 tablespoons olive oil
- Wooden or metal skewers, soaked in water if wooden

Instructions:

1. In a large bowl, combine the chopped onion, minced garlic, chopped cilantro, chopped parsley, ground cumin, ground coriander, ground cinnamon, ground paprika, ground turmeric, ground ginger, cayenne pepper, salt, black pepper, and olive oil. Mix well to form a marinade.
2. Add the cubed lamb to the marinade, tossing to coat the meat evenly. Cover the bowl and refrigerate for at least 1 hour, or overnight for best results, to allow the flavors to meld together.
3. Preheat your campfire or grill to medium-high heat, ensuring you have a bed of hot coals or an even flame.
4. Thread the marinated lamb cubes onto the skewers, leaving a little space between each piece to ensure even cooking.
5. Once the grill or campfire is ready, place the skewers directly onto the grate.
6. Grill the Moroccan Spiced Lamb Kebabs for about 8-10 minutes, turning occasionally, or until the meat is cooked to your desired level of doneness and has developed a nice char on the outside.
7. Once cooked, remove the kebabs from the grill and let them rest for a few minutes before serving.
8. Serve the Moroccan Spiced Lamb Kebabs hot, garnished with additional fresh cilantro and parsley if desired.
9. Enjoy your flavorful and aromatic Moroccan Spiced Lamb Kebabs as a delicious main dish at your next outdoor gathering!

Feel free to serve the kebabs with couscous, grilled vegetables, or a fresh salad for a complete meal.

**Coconut Curry Lentil Soup**

Ingredients:

- 1 tablespoon coconut oil or olive oil
- 1 onion, diced
- 3 cloves garlic, minced
- 1 tablespoon grated ginger
- 2 carrots, diced
- 2 celery stalks, diced
- 1 bell pepper (any color), diced
- 1 cup (200g) dried red lentils, rinsed and drained
- 1 can (14 ounces) coconut milk
- 4 cups (960ml) vegetable broth
- 2 teaspoons curry powder
- 1 teaspoon ground cumin
- 1/2 teaspoon ground turmeric
- 1/2 teaspoon paprika
- Salt and black pepper, to taste
- Juice of 1 lime
- Fresh cilantro, chopped, for garnish (optional)

Instructions:

1. Heat the coconut oil or olive oil in a large pot over medium heat, either on a campfire grate or a camp stove.
2. Add the diced onion to the pot and cook until softened, about 5 minutes.
3. Stir in the minced garlic and grated ginger, and cook for another minute until fragrant.
4. Add the diced carrots, celery, and bell pepper to the pot. Cook, stirring occasionally, for about 5 minutes, or until the vegetables start to soften.
5. Stir in the rinsed red lentils, coconut milk, vegetable broth, curry powder, ground cumin, ground turmeric, and paprika. Season with salt and black pepper to taste.
6. Bring the soup to a simmer, then reduce the heat to low. Cover the pot and let the soup cook for about 20-25 minutes, or until the lentils are tender and the vegetables are cooked through, stirring occasionally.
7. Once the soup is cooked, remove it from the heat. Stir in the lime juice.
8. Taste the soup and adjust the seasoning as needed, adding more salt, pepper, or lime juice if desired.
9. Ladle the Coconut Curry Lentil Soup into bowls and garnish with chopped fresh cilantro, if using.
10. Serve the soup hot and enjoy its comforting flavors while camping in the great outdoors!

Feel free to customize the soup by adding other vegetables such as spinach, kale, or potatoes. You can also adjust the spices to suit your taste preferences.

**Campfire Brie with Honey and Almonds**

Ingredients:

- 1 round of Brie cheese
- 2 tablespoons honey
- 1/4 cup sliced almonds
- Baguette slices or crackers, for serving

Instructions:

1. Preheat your campfire or grill to medium heat, ensuring you have a bed of hot coals or an even flame.
2. Place the round of Brie cheese in the center of a piece of heavy-duty aluminum foil, large enough to wrap around the cheese completely.
3. Drizzle the honey evenly over the top of the Brie cheese.
4. Sprinkle the sliced almonds over the honey-drizzled Brie cheese, pressing them gently into the cheese to adhere.
5. Carefully wrap the aluminum foil around the Brie cheese, ensuring it's sealed tightly to prevent any leakage.
6. Place the wrapped Brie cheese on the campfire grate or directly onto the hot coals. Cook for 8-10 minutes, or until the cheese is soft and gooey, and the honey and almonds are caramelized.
7. Carefully remove the wrapped Brie cheese from the campfire using heatproof gloves or oven mitts.
8. Unwrap the foil and transfer the Brie cheese to a serving platter.
9. Serve the Campfire Brie with Honey and Almonds hot, alongside baguette slices or crackers for dipping.
10. Enjoy the gooey, sweet, and nutty flavors of the Campfire Brie with Honey and Almonds as a delicious appetizer while enjoying the great outdoors!

Feel free to customize the toppings by adding dried fruits, such as cranberries or apricots, or fresh herbs, such as rosemary or thyme, for added flavor and aroma.

**Grilled Portobello Mushroom Burgers**

Ingredients:

- 4 large Portobello mushroom caps
- 1/4 cup balsamic vinegar
- 2 tablespoons olive oil
- 2 cloves garlic, minced
- 1 teaspoon dried thyme
- Salt and black pepper, to taste
- 4 burger buns
- Toppings of your choice (lettuce, tomato, onion, avocado, cheese, etc.)

Instructions:

1. Preheat your grill or campfire to medium-high heat, ensuring you have a bed of hot coals or an even flame.
2. In a small bowl, whisk together the balsamic vinegar, olive oil, minced garlic, dried thyme, salt, and black pepper to create a marinade.
3. Clean the Portobello mushroom caps by gently wiping them with a damp paper towel to remove any dirt. Remove the stems if they are still attached.
4. Place the mushroom caps in a shallow dish or a resealable plastic bag. Pour the marinade over the mushrooms, making sure they are evenly coated. Allow the mushrooms to marinate for at least 15-20 minutes, flipping them halfway through to ensure both sides are coated.
5. Once marinated, remove the mushrooms from the marinade and place them directly on the preheated grill or campfire grate, gill side down. Reserve the remaining marinade for basting.
6. Grill the mushrooms for 4-5 minutes on each side, or until they are tender and slightly charred, basting occasionally with the reserved marinade.
7. While the mushrooms are grilling, you can also toast the burger buns on the grill for a minute or two, if desired.
8. Once the mushrooms are cooked through, remove them from the grill and assemble your burgers. Place each grilled Portobello mushroom cap on a burger bun and top with your favorite toppings, such as lettuce, tomato, onion, avocado, and cheese.
9. Serve the Grilled Portobello Mushroom Burgers immediately, while still warm, and enjoy their hearty and flavorful goodness!

Feel free to customize your burgers with additional toppings and condiments to suit your taste preferences. These Grilled Portobello Mushroom Burgers are a delicious and satisfying option for vegetarians and meat-lovers alike!

**Campfire Tacos with Homemade Guacamole**

Ingredients for Tacos:

- 1 pound (about 450g) ground beef or turkey (or protein of your choice)
- 1 packet of taco seasoning mix (or homemade taco seasoning)
- 8-10 small corn or flour tortillas
- Toppings of your choice (shredded lettuce, diced tomatoes, diced onions, shredded cheese, salsa, sour cream, etc.)

Ingredients for Homemade Guacamole:

- 2 ripe avocados
- 1 small tomato, diced
- 1/4 cup diced onion
- 1 clove garlic, minced
- Juice of 1 lime
- Salt and pepper, to taste
- Optional: chopped cilantro, diced jalapeño for extra spice

Instructions:

1. Prepare your campfire or grill for medium heat, ensuring you have a bed of hot coals or an even flame.
2. In a skillet or Dutch oven, cook the ground beef or turkey over the campfire until it's browned and cooked through. Drain any excess fat.
3. Add the taco seasoning mix to the cooked meat according to the package instructions, or use your own homemade taco seasoning blend. Stir well to combine and let it simmer for a few minutes to allow the flavors to meld.
4. While the meat is cooking, prepare the homemade guacamole. In a bowl, mash the ripe avocados with a fork until smooth or chunky, depending on your preference.
5. Add the diced tomato, diced onion, minced garlic, lime juice, salt, pepper, and any optional ingredients like chopped cilantro or diced jalapeño. Mix until well combined.
6. Once the taco meat is ready and the guacamole is prepared, warm the tortillas over the campfire for about 30 seconds on each side, until they are heated through and slightly charred.
7. Assemble your Campfire Tacos by spooning some of the taco meat onto each warm tortilla, then topping it with a spoonful of homemade guacamole and any other toppings of your choice.
8. Serve the Campfire Tacos immediately and enjoy the delicious flavors of the outdoors!

These Campfire Tacos with Homemade Guacamole are customizable to suit your preferences, and they're sure to be a hit with everyone around the campfire!

**Foil Packet Lemon Herb Chicken**

Ingredients:

- 4 boneless, skinless chicken breasts
- 2 lemons, thinly sliced
- 4 cloves garlic, minced
- 2 tablespoons olive oil
- 2 tablespoons fresh herbs (such as rosemary, thyme, and parsley), chopped
- Salt and black pepper, to taste
- Optional: additional herbs for garnish

Instructions:

1. Preheat your campfire or grill to medium-high heat, ensuring you have a bed of hot coals or an even flame.
2. Cut four large pieces of heavy-duty aluminum foil, each large enough to wrap around one chicken breast and some lemon slices.
3. Place one chicken breast in the center of each piece of foil.
4. Drizzle olive oil over each chicken breast, then sprinkle minced garlic, chopped herbs, salt, and black pepper evenly over the chicken.
5. Place 2-3 slices of lemon on top of each chicken breast.
6. Fold the foil over the chicken to create a packet, ensuring it's sealed tightly to prevent any juices from leaking out during cooking.
7. Place the foil packets directly onto the preheated grill grate or campfire coals.
8. Cook the foil packets for about 15-20 minutes, flipping halfway through, or until the chicken is cooked through and reaches an internal temperature of 165°F (75°C).
9. Carefully remove the foil packets from the heat using tongs or heatproof gloves.
10. Open the foil packets carefully to avoid burning yourself with the steam.
11. Transfer the chicken breasts to serving plates and garnish with additional fresh herbs, if desired.
12. Serve the Foil Packet Lemon Herb Chicken hot, with your favorite sides such as rice, roasted vegetables, or a salad.

Enjoy the juicy and flavorful Foil Packet Lemon Herb Chicken, perfect for a camping meal under the stars!

**Dutch Oven Lasagna**

Ingredients:

- 1 pound (450g) ground beef or Italian sausage
- 1 onion, diced
- 3 cloves garlic, minced
- 1 can (28 ounces) crushed tomatoes
- 1 can (6 ounces) tomato paste
- 2 teaspoons dried basil
- 1 teaspoon dried oregano
- Salt and black pepper, to taste
- 9 lasagna noodles, uncooked
- 2 cups (200g) shredded mozzarella cheese
- 1 cup (100g) grated Parmesan cheese
- Fresh basil leaves, for garnish (optional)

Instructions:

1. Heat a Dutch oven over medium heat, either on a campfire grate or a camp stove.
2. Add the ground beef or Italian sausage to the Dutch oven and cook until browned, breaking it up with a spoon as it cooks.
3. Add the diced onion and minced garlic to the Dutch oven with the browned meat. Cook until the onion is softened and translucent, about 5 minutes.
4. Stir in the crushed tomatoes, tomato paste, dried basil, dried oregano, salt, and black pepper. Mix well to combine all the ingredients.
5. Break the lasagna noodles into pieces that will fit into the Dutch oven. Arrange a layer of noodles over the meat sauce in the Dutch oven.
6. Spread a layer of the shredded mozzarella cheese over the noodles, followed by a layer of the grated Parmesan cheese.
7. Repeat the layers of noodles, meat sauce, and cheese until all the ingredients are used up, finishing with a layer of cheese on top.
8. Cover the Dutch oven with its lid and place it over the campfire grate or directly onto the hot coals.
9. Cook the Dutch Oven Lasagna for about 45-60 minutes, or until the noodles are cooked through and the cheese is melted and bubbly, checking occasionally to ensure it doesn't burn on the bottom.

10. Once cooked, remove the Dutch oven from the heat using heatproof gloves or oven mitts.
11. Let the Dutch Oven Lasagna cool for a few minutes before serving. Garnish with fresh basil leaves, if desired.
12. Serve the lasagna directly from the Dutch oven, scooping out generous portions onto plates or into bowls.

Enjoy your delicious and comforting Dutch Oven Lasagna, perfect for a cozy camping meal!

**Campfire Banana S'mores**

Ingredients:

- Ripe bananas
- Chocolate bars (such as milk chocolate or dark chocolate), broken into pieces
- Marshmallows
- Graham crackers, broken into squares

Instructions:

1. Preheat your campfire to medium heat, ensuring you have a bed of hot coals or an even flame.
2. Peel the bananas and slice them lengthwise, leaving the peel on one side intact (similar to a hot dog bun).
3. Place a few pieces of chocolate onto the cut side of one banana half.
4. Place a marshmallow on top of the chocolate.
5. Place the other banana half on top, creating a banana "sandwich" with the chocolate and marshmallow in the middle. Use the peel to wrap the banana sandwich, securing it closed.
6. Repeat the process with the remaining bananas, chocolate, and marshmallows.
7. Carefully wrap each banana sandwich in aluminum foil, ensuring they are sealed tightly.
8. Place the foil-wrapped banana sandwiches onto the campfire grate or directly onto the hot coals.
9. Cook the banana sandwiches for 5-7 minutes, flipping them occasionally with tongs to ensure even cooking.
10. Once the bananas are soft and the chocolate and marshmallows are melted, carefully remove them from the campfire using heatproof gloves or oven mitts.
11. Unwrap the foil from each banana sandwich and transfer them to serving plates.
12. Serve the Campfire Banana S'mores with graham crackers for dipping or as a side, allowing everyone to scoop out the gooey goodness with their crackers.

Enjoy your delicious and fun Campfire Banana S'mores, perfect for a sweet treat around the campfire!

**Cajun Shrimp Foil Packets**

Ingredients:

- 1 pound (about 450g) large shrimp, peeled and deveined
- 2-3 tablespoons Cajun seasoning (adjust to taste)
- 2 tablespoons olive oil
- 1 bell pepper, thinly sliced
- 1 small onion, thinly sliced
- 1 zucchini, thinly sliced
- 2 cloves garlic, minced
- Salt and black pepper, to taste
- Fresh parsley, chopped, for garnish (optional)
- Lemon wedges, for serving

Instructions:

1. Preheat your campfire or grill to medium-high heat, ensuring you have a bed of hot coals or an even flame.
2. In a large bowl, toss the peeled and deveined shrimp with Cajun seasoning and olive oil until evenly coated. Set aside.
3. Cut four large pieces of heavy-duty aluminum foil, each large enough to wrap around one serving of shrimp and vegetables.
4. Divide the sliced bell pepper, onion, zucchini, and minced garlic evenly among the foil packets, placing them in the center of each piece of foil.
5. Season the vegetables with salt and black pepper to taste.
6. Place an equal portion of seasoned shrimp on top of the vegetables in each foil packet.
7. Fold the sides of the foil over the shrimp and vegetables to create a packet, ensuring it's sealed tightly to prevent any juices from leaking out during cooking.
8. Place the foil packets directly onto the preheated grill grate or campfire coals.
9. Cook the foil packets for about 10-12 minutes, flipping halfway through, or until the shrimp are pink and opaque, and the vegetables are tender.
10. Carefully remove the foil packets from the heat using tongs or heatproof gloves.
11. Open the foil packets carefully to avoid burning yourself with the steam.
12. Sprinkle the Cajun Shrimp Foil Packets with chopped fresh parsley for garnish, if desired.
13. Serve the foil packets hot, with lemon wedges on the side for squeezing over the shrimp and vegetables.

Enjoy your flavorful and aromatic Cajun Shrimp Foil Packets, perfect for a hassle-free camping meal!

**Skillet Sausage and Potato Hash**

Ingredients:

- 1 pound (about 450g) smoked sausage or kielbasa, sliced into rounds
- 1 onion, diced
- 2 cloves garlic, minced
- 3-4 medium potatoes, diced into small cubes
- 1 bell pepper, diced
- 2 tablespoons olive oil or cooking oil of your choice
- 1 teaspoon paprika
- 1/2 teaspoon dried thyme
- Salt and black pepper, to taste
- Fresh parsley, chopped, for garnish (optional)
- Eggs, cooked to your liking (optional, for serving)

Instructions:

1. Heat a cast iron skillet or large skillet over medium heat, either on a campfire grate or a camp stove.
2. Add the sliced smoked sausage or kielbasa to the skillet and cook until browned and slightly crispy, about 5-7 minutes. Remove the sausage from the skillet and set aside.
3. In the same skillet, add the diced onion and cook until softened and translucent, about 3-4 minutes.
4. Add the minced garlic to the skillet and cook for another minute until fragrant.
5. Add the diced potatoes to the skillet, spreading them out into an even layer. Let them cook without stirring for a few minutes to allow them to brown on one side.
6. Stir the potatoes and continue to cook until they are golden brown and slightly crispy on all sides, about 8-10 minutes.
7. Add the diced bell pepper to the skillet and cook for another 3-4 minutes, until softened.
8. Return the cooked sausage to the skillet and stir to combine with the potatoes and bell pepper.
9. Sprinkle the paprika and dried thyme over the sausage and potato mixture. Season with salt and black pepper to taste.
10. Cook everything together for an additional 2-3 minutes, stirring occasionally to ensure even cooking and to allow the flavors to meld.
11. Once everything is cooked through and well combined, remove the skillet from the heat.
12. Garnish the Skillet Sausage and Potato Hash with chopped fresh parsley, if desired.
13. Serve the hash hot, with cooked eggs on top if desired, for a delicious and hearty camping breakfast or brunch!

Enjoy your flavorful and satisfying Skillet Sausage and Potato Hash, perfect for fueling your outdoor adventures!

**Campfire Garlic Butter Lobster Tails**

Ingredients:

- 4 lobster tails, thawed if frozen
- 1/2 cup (115g) unsalted butter, melted
- 4 cloves garlic, minced
- 2 tablespoons fresh parsley, chopped
- Salt and black pepper, to taste
- Lemon wedges, for serving

Instructions:

1. Preheat your campfire or grill to medium-high heat, ensuring you have a bed of hot coals or an even flame.
2. Use kitchen shears or a sharp knife to carefully cut along the top of each lobster tail shell, stopping at the tail. Gently pull apart the shell to expose the meat, leaving it attached at the tail.
3. In a small bowl, mix together the melted butter, minced garlic, chopped parsley, salt, and black pepper.
4. Brush the garlic butter mixture generously over the exposed lobster meat, making sure to coat it evenly.
5. Once the campfire or grill is ready, place the prepared lobster tails directly onto the grate, meat side down.
6. Cook the lobster tails for 5-7 minutes, then carefully flip them over using tongs.
7. Continue to cook the lobster tails for an additional 5-7 minutes, or until the meat is opaque and cooked through, and the shells are bright red.
8. Once cooked, carefully remove the lobster tails from the heat using tongs or a spatula.
9. Serve the Campfire Garlic Butter Lobster Tails hot, with lemon wedges on the side for squeezing over the lobster meat.
10. Enjoy the luxurious and flavorful Campfire Garlic Butter Lobster Tails as a decadent treat while enjoying the great outdoors!

These lobster tails are sure to impress your fellow campers with their rich flavor and succulent meat.

Make sure to have plenty of napkins on hand for messy fingers!

**Campfire Quesadillas with Caramelized Onions**

Ingredients:

- Flour tortillas
- Shredded cheese (such as cheddar, Monterey Jack, or a Mexican cheese blend)
- Caramelized onions (see instructions below)
- Optional additional fillings: cooked chicken, cooked steak, sautéed bell peppers, sautéed mushrooms, black beans, corn, etc.
- Cooking oil or butter, for greasing the skillet

Instructions for Caramelized Onions:

1. Thinly slice 2-3 onions.
2. Heat a skillet over medium-low heat, either on a campfire grate or a camp stove.
3. Add a drizzle of cooking oil or a pat of butter to the skillet.
4. Add the sliced onions to the skillet and cook, stirring occasionally, for about 20-30 minutes, or until the onions are soft, golden brown, and caramelized.
5. Once caramelized, remove the onions from the skillet and set aside.

Instructions for Campfire Quesadillas:

1. Preheat a cast iron skillet or griddle over medium heat, either on a campfire grate or a camp stove.
2. Place one flour tortilla in the skillet and sprinkle a generous amount of shredded cheese evenly over the tortilla.
3. Add a layer of caramelized onions (and any additional fillings, if using) over half of the tortilla.
4. Fold the other half of the tortilla over the filling to create a half-moon shape.
5. Cook the quesadilla for 2-3 minutes on each side, or until the tortilla is golden brown and crispy, and the cheese is melted and gooey.
6. Repeat the process with the remaining tortillas and fillings.
7. Once cooked, remove the quesadillas from the skillet and let them cool for a minute before slicing.
8. Slice each quesadilla into wedges and serve hot.
9. Enjoy your delicious Campfire Quesadillas with Caramelized Onions as a tasty and satisfying camping meal!

These quesadillas are customizable, so feel free to add or omit fillings based on your preferences. They're perfect for enjoying around the campfire with friends and family.

**Dutch Oven Chicken Cacciatore**

Ingredients:

- 4 chicken leg quarters or 8 chicken thighs, bone-in and skin-on
- Salt and black pepper, to taste
- 2 tablespoons olive oil
- 1 onion, diced
- 2 cloves garlic, minced
- 1 bell pepper, diced
- 8 ounces (225g) mushrooms, sliced
- 1 can (14 ounces) diced tomatoes, undrained
- 1 can (6 ounces) tomato paste
- 1/2 cup (120ml) dry red wine (such as Chianti or Merlot)
- 1 teaspoon dried oregano
- 1 teaspoon dried basil
- 1 teaspoon dried thyme
- 1/2 teaspoon red pepper flakes (optional, for heat)
- Fresh parsley, chopped, for garnish (optional)

Instructions:

1. Season the chicken leg quarters or thighs generously with salt and black pepper.
2. Heat a Dutch oven over medium-high heat, either on a campfire grate or a camp stove. Add the olive oil to the Dutch oven.
3. Once the oil is hot, add the chicken pieces to the Dutch oven, skin side down. Cook until the chicken is golden brown and crispy on both sides, about 5-7 minutes per side. Remove the chicken from the Dutch oven and set aside.
4. In the same Dutch oven, add the diced onion, minced garlic, diced bell pepper, and sliced mushrooms. Cook, stirring occasionally, until the vegetables are softened and the mushrooms have released their juices, about 5-7 minutes.
5. Stir in the diced tomatoes (with their juices) and tomato paste, scraping up any browned bits from the bottom of the Dutch oven.
6. Add the dry red wine, dried oregano, dried basil, dried thyme, and red pepper flakes (if using). Stir to combine.
7. Return the browned chicken pieces to the Dutch oven, nestling them into the sauce.
8. Cover the Dutch oven with its lid and place it over the campfire grate or directly onto the hot coals.
9. Cook the Dutch Oven Chicken Cacciatore for about 45-60 minutes, or until the chicken is cooked through and tender, and the sauce has thickened, stirring occasionally.
10. Once cooked, remove the Dutch oven from the heat.
11. Garnish the Chicken Cacciatore with chopped fresh parsley, if desired.

12. Serve the Chicken Cacciatore hot, spooned over cooked pasta, rice, or polenta, and enjoy its rich and flavorful goodness!

This Dutch Oven Chicken Cacciatore is sure to be a hit with everyone around the campfire. It's comforting, satisfying, and perfect for outdoor gatherings.

**Campfire Ratatouille**

Ingredients:

- 1 eggplant, diced
- 2 zucchini, diced
- 2 bell peppers, diced
- 1 onion, diced
- 2 cloves garlic, minced
- 4 tomatoes, diced
- 2 tablespoons tomato paste
- 2 tablespoons olive oil
- 1 teaspoon dried thyme
- 1 teaspoon dried oregano
- Salt and black pepper, to taste
- Fresh basil, chopped, for garnish (optional)

Instructions:

1. Prepare your campfire or grill for medium heat, ensuring you have a bed of hot coals or an even flame.
2. Heat a cast iron skillet or Dutch oven over the campfire or grill, then add the olive oil.
3. Add the diced onion and minced garlic to the skillet, and cook until softened and fragrant, about 3-4 minutes.
4. Add the diced eggplant, zucchini, and bell peppers to the skillet, stirring to combine with the onion and garlic.
5. Cook the vegetables until they begin to soften, stirring occasionally, about 5-7 minutes.
6. Add the diced tomatoes and tomato paste to the skillet, stirring to combine with the vegetables.
7. Season the ratatouille with dried thyme, dried oregano, salt, and black pepper, to taste. Stir well to incorporate the seasoning.
8. Cover the skillet or Dutch oven with a lid and let the ratatouille simmer over the campfire or grill for about 20-25 minutes, stirring occasionally, until the vegetables are tender and the flavors have melded together.
9. Once cooked, remove the skillet or Dutch oven from the heat.
10. Garnish the Campfire Ratatouille with chopped fresh basil, if desired, before serving.
11. Serve the ratatouille hot as a side dish or main course, accompanied by crusty bread or cooked grains, such as rice or quinoa.

Enjoy the rustic and comforting flavors of Campfire Ratatouille, perfect for a cozy evening around the campfire!

**Foil Packet Teriyaki Salmon**

Ingredients:

- 4 salmon fillets (about 6 ounces each)
- 1/4 cup soy sauce
- 2 tablespoons honey
- 2 tablespoons rice vinegar
- 1 tablespoon sesame oil
- 2 cloves garlic, minced
- 1 teaspoon grated fresh ginger
- 1 green onion, thinly sliced (optional, for garnish)
- Sesame seeds, for garnish (optional)
- Sliced green onions, for garnish (optional)

Instructions:

1. Preheat your campfire or grill to medium heat, ensuring you have a bed of hot coals or an even flame.
2. In a small bowl, whisk together the soy sauce, honey, rice vinegar, sesame oil, minced garlic, and grated ginger to make the teriyaki sauce.
3. Cut four large pieces of heavy-duty aluminum foil, each large enough to wrap around one salmon fillet with some extra space.
4. Place one salmon fillet in the center of each piece of foil.
5. Pour the teriyaki sauce evenly over each salmon fillet, ensuring they are coated on all sides.
6. Fold the sides of the foil over the salmon to create a packet, sealing it tightly to prevent any juices from leaking out during cooking.
7. Place the foil packets directly onto the preheated grill grate or campfire coals.
8. Cook the foil packets for about 10-12 minutes, or until the salmon is cooked through and flakes easily with a fork.
9. Once cooked, carefully remove the foil packets from the heat using tongs or heatproof gloves.
10. Carefully open the foil packets, taking care to avoid the steam.
11. Transfer the salmon fillets to serving plates.
12. Garnish the Foil Packet Teriyaki Salmon with sliced green onions and sesame seeds, if desired.
13. Serve the salmon hot, accompanied by your favorite side dishes, such as rice and steamed vegetables.

Enjoy the delicious and flavorful Foil Packet Teriyaki Salmon as a satisfying camping meal!

**Grilled Peach and Burrata Salad**

Ingredients:

- 2 ripe peaches, halved and pitted
- 1 tablespoon olive oil
- Salt and black pepper, to taste
- 4 cups mixed salad greens (such as arugula, spinach, or mixed baby greens)
- 1 ball of burrata cheese
- Balsamic glaze, for drizzling
- Fresh basil leaves, torn, for garnish (optional)
- Toasted pine nuts or walnuts, for garnish (optional)

Instructions:

1. Preheat your grill or campfire to medium heat.
2. Brush the cut side of each peach half with olive oil and season with salt and black pepper.
3. Place the peach halves on the grill, cut side down, and cook for 3-4 minutes, or until grill marks appear and the peaches are slightly softened.
4. Flip the peaches over and grill for an additional 2-3 minutes on the skin side. Remove from the grill and let cool slightly.
5. While the peaches are cooling, arrange the mixed salad greens on a serving platter or individual plates.
6. Tear the burrata cheese into pieces and scatter it over the salad greens.
7. Once the grilled peaches are cool enough to handle, slice them into wedges and arrange them over the salad.
8. Drizzle the salad with balsamic glaze.
9. Garnish the Grilled Peach and Burrata Salad with torn basil leaves and toasted pine nuts or walnuts, if desired.
10. Serve the salad immediately, while the peaches and burrata are still warm from the grill, and enjoy the combination of flavors and textures.

This Grilled Peach and Burrata Salad is perfect for summer gatherings or as a light and elegant dish to enjoy while camping. The sweetness of the grilled peaches complements the creamy burrata cheese beautifully, making it a memorable and satisfying salad.

**Campfire Stuffed Peppers with Sausage and Rice**

Ingredients:

- 4 large bell peppers (any color), halved and seeds removed
- 1 pound (about 450g) Italian sausage, casings removed
- 1 cup cooked rice (white or brown)
- 1 small onion, finely chopped
- 2 cloves garlic, minced
- 1 can (14.5 ounces) diced tomatoes, drained
- 1 cup shredded mozzarella cheese
- 2 tablespoons olive oil
- Salt and black pepper, to taste
- Fresh parsley, chopped, for garnish (optional)

Instructions:

1. Preheat your campfire or grill to medium heat, ensuring you have a bed of hot coals or an even flame.
2. Heat a skillet over the campfire or grill, then add the olive oil.
3. Add the Italian sausage to the skillet and cook until browned, breaking it up with a spoon as it cooks.
4. Add the chopped onion and minced garlic to the skillet with the sausage, and cook until the onion is softened and translucent, about 3-4 minutes.
5. Stir in the cooked rice and diced tomatoes, mixing until well combined with the sausage mixture. Cook for an additional 2-3 minutes to heat through.
6. Season the sausage and rice mixture with salt and black pepper, to taste. Remove the skillet from the heat.
7. Spoon the sausage and rice mixture evenly into each halved bell pepper, filling them to the top.
8. Place the stuffed peppers in a cast iron skillet or baking dish, arranging them so they fit snugly.
9. Sprinkle shredded mozzarella cheese over the tops of the stuffed peppers.
10. Cover the skillet or baking dish with aluminum foil.
11. Place the skillet or baking dish over the campfire or grill, and cook for about 25-30 minutes, or until the peppers are tender and the cheese is melted and bubbly.
12. Once cooked, carefully remove the skillet or baking dish from the heat using heatproof gloves or oven mitts.
13. Garnish the Campfire Stuffed Peppers with chopped fresh parsley, if desired.
14. Serve the stuffed peppers hot, and enjoy the hearty and flavorful combination of sausage, rice, and melted cheese!

These Campfire Stuffed Peppers with Sausage and Rice are sure to be a hit with everyone around the campfire. They're easy to make and packed with delicious flavors, making them perfect for a satisfying camping meal.

**Dutch Oven Lemon Herb Roast Chicken**

Ingredients:

- 1 whole chicken (about 4-5 pounds)
- 2 lemons, halved
- 4 cloves garlic, minced
- 2 tablespoons olive oil
- 2 tablespoons fresh herbs (such as rosemary, thyme, and parsley), chopped
- Salt and black pepper, to taste
- 1 onion, quartered
- 2 carrots, chopped into large pieces
- 2 celery stalks, chopped into large pieces
- 1 cup chicken broth or water

Instructions:

1. Prepare your campfire by setting up a ring of hot coals around the perimeter, leaving an empty space in the center for your Dutch oven.
2. Season the whole chicken generously with salt and black pepper, both inside and out.
3. Stuff the cavity of the chicken with the halved lemons, minced garlic, and chopped fresh herbs.
4. Tie the legs of the chicken together with kitchen twine to help it cook evenly.
5. Heat a Dutch oven over the campfire, either directly on the hot coals or on a campfire grate.
6. Add the olive oil to the Dutch oven and heat it until shimmering.
7. Place the seasoned and stuffed chicken into the Dutch oven, breast side up.
8. Arrange the quartered onion, chopped carrots, and chopped celery around the chicken in the Dutch oven.
9. Pour the chicken broth or water into the Dutch oven around the chicken and vegetables.
10. Cover the Dutch oven with its lid and place hot coals on top of the lid to create an even cooking environment.
11. Cook the Dutch Oven Lemon Herb Roast Chicken for about 1.5 to 2 hours, or until the internal temperature of the thickest part of the chicken reaches 165°F (75°C), and the juices run clear when pierced with a knife.
12. Once cooked, carefully remove the Dutch oven from the heat using heatproof gloves or oven mitts.
13. Let the chicken rest for 10-15 minutes before carving.
14. Carve the chicken and serve it with the roasted vegetables and pan juices from the Dutch oven.

Enjoy the succulent and flavorful Dutch Oven Lemon Herb Roast Chicken, perfect for a cozy campfire meal with friends and family!

**Campfire Nachos with Homemade Pico de Gallo**

Ingredients:

For the Pico de Gallo:

- 4 tomatoes, diced
- 1 onion, finely chopped
- 1 jalapeño pepper, seeded and finely chopped
- 1/4 cup fresh cilantro, chopped
- Juice of 1 lime
- Salt and black pepper, to taste

For the Nachos:

- Tortilla chips
- Shredded cheese (such as cheddar, Monterey Jack, or a Mexican blend)
- Cooked protein of your choice (such as grilled chicken, ground beef, or black beans)
- Optional toppings: sliced black olives, diced avocado, sliced jalapeños, sour cream, guacamole, salsa, chopped green onions, chopped fresh cilantro, etc.

Instructions:

1. Prepare the Pico de Gallo by combining the diced tomatoes, chopped onion, chopped jalapeño pepper, chopped cilantro, lime juice, salt, and black pepper in a bowl. Mix well and set aside to allow the flavors to meld.
2. Preheat your campfire grill or a grill grate over medium heat.
3. Arrange a layer of tortilla chips on a large sheet of heavy-duty aluminum foil or a disposable aluminum pan.
4. Sprinkle a layer of shredded cheese over the tortilla chips, followed by your choice of cooked protein.
5. Add another layer of tortilla chips on top of the cheese and protein layer, followed by another layer of cheese and protein.
6. Continue layering the tortilla chips, cheese, and protein until you've used up all your ingredients, ending with a layer of cheese on top.
7. Carefully transfer the foil packet or aluminum pan to the preheated grill grate over the campfire.
8. Cook the Campfire Nachos for about 5-10 minutes, or until the cheese is melted and bubbly, and the nachos are heated through.

9. Once cooked, carefully remove the foil packet or aluminum pan from the grill using heatproof gloves or oven mitts.
10. Top the hot Campfire Nachos with spoonfuls of homemade Pico de Gallo and any other desired toppings, such as sliced black olives, diced avocado, sour cream, guacamole, salsa, sliced jalapeños, chopped green onions, or chopped fresh cilantro.
11. Serve the loaded Campfire Nachos immediately, and enjoy the cheesy, flavorful goodness!

These Campfire Nachos with Homemade Pico de Gallo are sure to be a hit at your camping gatherings. They're customizable, easy to make, and perfect for sharing around the campfire with friends and family.

**Foil Packet BBQ Ribs**

Ingredients:

- 2 racks of baby back ribs
- Your favorite BBQ sauce
- Salt and black pepper, to taste
- Optional: garlic powder, onion powder, paprika, or other seasonings of your choice

Instructions:

1. Preheat your campfire grill or a grill grate over medium heat.
2. Season the racks of baby back ribs generously with salt, black pepper, and any additional seasonings you like, such as garlic powder, onion powder, or paprika. Pat the seasonings into the meat to ensure they adhere well.
3. Tear off two large sheets of heavy-duty aluminum foil, each large enough to fully wrap around one rack of ribs.
4. Place one rack of ribs on each sheet of aluminum foil.
5. Brush both sides of each rack of ribs generously with your favorite BBQ sauce, making sure to coat them evenly.
6. Fold the sides of the foil over the ribs to create a packet, sealing it tightly to prevent any juices from leaking out during cooking.
7. Place the foil packets directly onto the preheated grill grate over the campfire.
8. Cook the Foil Packet BBQ Ribs for about 1.5 to 2 hours, flipping them occasionally, or until the meat is tender and pulls away easily from the bones.
9. Carefully remove the foil packets from the grill using heatproof gloves or oven mitts.
10. Carefully open the foil packets, taking care to avoid the steam.
11. Transfer the cooked ribs to a serving platter or cutting board.
12. Optional: Brush the ribs with additional BBQ sauce for extra flavor and shine.
13. Let the ribs rest for a few minutes before slicing them into individual portions.
14. Serve the Foil Packet BBQ Ribs hot, and enjoy the tender, flavorful meat with your favorite side dishes, such as coleslaw, cornbread, or grilled vegetables.

These Foil Packet BBQ Ribs are perfect for camping trips, backyard cookouts, or any outdoor gathering. They're easy to make, packed with flavor, and guaranteed to be a crowd-pleaser!

**Campfire Vegetable Curry**

Ingredients:

- 2 tablespoons vegetable oil
- 1 onion, diced
- 2 cloves garlic, minced
- 1 tablespoon fresh ginger, minced
- 2 tablespoons curry powder
- 1 teaspoon ground cumin
- 1 teaspoon ground coriander
- 1/2 teaspoon ground turmeric
- 1/4 teaspoon cayenne pepper (optional, for heat)
- 1 can (14 ounces) coconut milk
- 1 cup vegetable broth
- 2 large carrots, peeled and diced
- 2 medium potatoes, peeled and diced
- 1 bell pepper, diced
- 1 zucchini, diced
- 1 cup frozen peas
- Salt and black pepper, to taste
- Fresh cilantro, chopped, for garnish (optional)
- Cooked rice or naan bread, for serving

Instructions:

1. Heat the vegetable oil in a large Dutch oven or pot over medium heat, either on a campfire grate or a camp stove.
2. Add the diced onion to the pot and cook until softened and translucent, about 3-4 minutes.
3. Add the minced garlic and minced ginger to the pot, and cook for another minute until fragrant.
4. Stir in the curry powder, ground cumin, ground coriander, ground turmeric, and cayenne pepper (if using). Cook for another minute to toast the spices and release their flavors.
5. Pour in the coconut milk and vegetable broth, stirring to combine with the onion and spice mixture.
6. Add the diced carrots and potatoes to the pot, stirring to coat them in the curry sauce. Cover the pot and let the vegetables simmer for about 10 minutes, or until they start to soften.
7. Stir in the diced bell pepper, diced zucchini, and frozen peas. Cover the pot again and let the curry simmer for another 10-15 minutes, or until all the vegetables are tender and cooked through.
8. Season the Campfire Vegetable Curry with salt and black pepper, to taste.
9. Once cooked, remove the pot from the heat.

10. Serve the Campfire Vegetable Curry hot, garnished with chopped fresh cilantro, if desired.
11. Serve the curry with cooked rice or naan bread for a delicious and satisfying camping meal.

Enjoy the aromatic and flavorful Campfire Vegetable Curry, perfect for warming up on cool evenings in the great outdoors!

**Skillet Garlic Butter Steak**

Ingredients:

- 2 steaks of your choice (such as ribeye, sirloin, or filet mignon)
- Salt and black pepper, to taste
- 2 tablespoons olive oil or cooking oil of your choice
- 4 tablespoons unsalted butter
- 4 cloves garlic, minced
- Fresh herbs (such as rosemary or thyme), chopped (optional)
- Lemon wedges, for serving

Instructions:

1. Season the steaks generously with salt and black pepper on both sides.
2. Heat a cast iron skillet over medium-high heat, either on a campfire grate or a camp stove.
3. Add the olive oil to the skillet and heat it until shimmering.
4. Carefully place the seasoned steaks in the hot skillet and cook them for about 3-4 minutes on each side for medium-rare, or until they reach your desired level of doneness.
5. While the steaks are cooking, melt the butter in a small saucepan or skillet over low heat, either on a separate burner or on the campfire grate.
6. Once the butter is melted, add the minced garlic to the skillet and cook for 1-2 minutes, or until the garlic is fragrant and lightly golden brown. Be careful not to let the garlic burn.
7. Optional: Stir in the chopped fresh herbs (such as rosemary or thyme) into the garlic butter for extra flavor.
8. Once the steaks are cooked to your liking, remove them from the skillet and transfer them to a plate or cutting board.
9. Pour the garlic butter over the cooked steaks, making sure to coat them evenly.
10. Let the steaks rest for a few minutes before slicing or serving.
11. Serve the Skillet Garlic Butter Steak hot, with lemon wedges on the side for squeezing over the steak for extra flavor.
12. Enjoy your delicious and flavorful Skillet Garlic Butter Steak, perfect for a satisfying camping meal!

This Skillet Garlic Butter Steak is sure to be a hit with everyone around the campfire. It's simple to make, yet packed with flavor, making it a great option for camping dinners.

**Dutch Oven Vegetable Soup**

Ingredients:

- 2 tablespoons olive oil
- 1 onion, diced
- 2 carrots, diced
- 2 celery stalks, diced
- 2 cloves garlic, minced
- 1 potato, peeled and diced
- 1 zucchini, diced
- 1 cup green beans, trimmed and cut into bite-sized pieces
- 1 can (14.5 ounces) diced tomatoes, undrained
- 4 cups vegetable broth
- 1 teaspoon dried thyme
- 1 teaspoon dried oregano
- Salt and black pepper, to taste
- Fresh parsley, chopped, for garnish (optional)

Instructions:

1. Heat the olive oil in a Dutch oven over medium heat, either on a campfire grate or a camp stove.
2. Add the diced onion, carrots, and celery to the Dutch oven, and cook until the vegetables are softened, about 5-7 minutes.
3. Add the minced garlic to the Dutch oven and cook for another minute until fragrant.
4. Stir in the diced potato, zucchini, and green beans, and cook for another 2-3 minutes.
5. Add the diced tomatoes (with their juices) and vegetable broth to the Dutch oven, stirring to combine.
6. Season the vegetable soup with dried thyme, dried oregano, salt, and black pepper, to taste. Stir well to incorporate the seasonings.
7. Cover the Dutch oven with its lid and let the soup simmer over medium-low heat for about 20-25 minutes, or until the vegetables are tender.
8. Once the soup is cooked, taste and adjust the seasoning if necessary.
9. Ladle the Dutch Oven Vegetable Soup into bowls and garnish with chopped fresh parsley, if desired.
10. Serve the soup hot, accompanied by crusty bread or dinner rolls for dipping.

Enjoy the comforting and nourishing Dutch Oven Vegetable Soup as a delicious meal during your camping adventures!

**Campfire Macaroni and Cheese**

Ingredients:

- 8 ounces (about 2 cups) elbow macaroni or your favorite pasta shape
- 2 tablespoons unsalted butter
- 2 tablespoons all-purpose flour
- 2 cups milk
- 2 cups shredded cheese (such as cheddar, Monterey Jack, or a blend)
- Salt and black pepper, to taste
- Optional mix-ins: cooked bacon, diced ham, cooked chicken, chopped vegetables, etc.
- Optional toppings: breadcrumbs, grated Parmesan cheese, chopped fresh herbs, etc.

Instructions:

1. Cook the elbow macaroni or pasta according to the package instructions until al dente. Drain and set aside.
2. Heat a cast iron skillet or Dutch oven over medium heat, either on a campfire grate or a camp stove.
3. Melt the unsalted butter in the skillet or Dutch oven.
4. Once the butter is melted, add the all-purpose flour to the skillet or Dutch oven, stirring to combine and form a roux. Cook the roux for 1-2 minutes, stirring constantly, until it turns golden brown and fragrant.
5. Gradually pour the milk into the skillet or Dutch oven, whisking constantly to prevent lumps from forming.
6. Cook the milk mixture, stirring constantly, until it thickens and starts to bubble, about 3-5 minutes.
7. Reduce the heat to low, and stir in the shredded cheese until melted and smooth.
8. Season the cheese sauce with salt and black pepper, to taste.
9. Stir in any optional mix-ins you desire, such as cooked bacon, diced ham, cooked chicken, or chopped vegetables.
10. Add the cooked macaroni or pasta to the cheese sauce in the skillet or Dutch oven, stirring until well coated.
11. If desired, sprinkle breadcrumbs, grated Parmesan cheese, or chopped fresh herbs over the top of the macaroni and cheese.
12. Cover the skillet or Dutch oven with its lid and let the macaroni and cheese cook over low heat for a few minutes to allow the flavors to meld together.
13. Once heated through, remove the skillet or Dutch oven from the heat.
14. Serve the Campfire Macaroni and Cheese hot, and enjoy its creamy and cheesy goodness!

This Campfire Macaroni and Cheese is sure to be a hit with everyone around the campfire. It's easy to make and incredibly satisfying, making it the perfect comfort food for outdoor adventures.

**Foil Packet Mediterranean Salmon**

Ingredients:

- 2 salmon fillets (about 6 ounces each)
- 1 tablespoon olive oil
- 2 cloves garlic, minced
- 1 teaspoon dried oregano
- 1/2 teaspoon dried thyme
- 1/2 teaspoon dried basil
- 1/4 teaspoon dried rosemary
- Salt and black pepper, to taste
- 1/2 cup cherry tomatoes, halved
- 1/4 cup Kalamata olives, pitted and halved
- 1/4 cup artichoke hearts, quartered
- 1/4 cup crumbled feta cheese
- Lemon wedges, for serving
- Fresh parsley, chopped, for garnish (optional)

Instructions:

1. Preheat your campfire grill or a grill grate over medium heat.
2. Tear off two large sheets of heavy-duty aluminum foil, each large enough to fully wrap around one salmon fillet with some extra space.
3. Place one salmon fillet in the center of each piece of foil.
4. Drizzle olive oil over each salmon fillet.
5. Sprinkle minced garlic, dried oregano, dried thyme, dried basil, dried rosemary, salt, and black pepper over each salmon fillet, distributing the seasonings evenly.
6. Top each salmon fillet with halved cherry tomatoes, halved Kalamata olives, quartered artichoke hearts, and crumbled feta cheese.
7. Fold the sides of the foil over the salmon to create a packet, sealing it tightly to prevent any juices from leaking out during cooking.
8. Place the foil packets directly onto the preheated grill grate over the campfire.
9. Cook the Foil Packet Mediterranean Salmon for about 10-15 minutes, or until the salmon is cooked through and flakes easily with a fork.
10. Once cooked, carefully remove the foil packets from the grill using tongs or heatproof gloves.
11. Carefully open the foil packets, taking care to avoid the steam.
12. Serve the Foil Packet Mediterranean Salmon hot, garnished with fresh parsley and lemon wedges on the side.
13. Enjoy the flavorful and healthy Mediterranean-inspired salmon, perfect for a satisfying camping meal!

This Foil Packet Mediterranean Salmon is easy to make and packed with delicious flavors from the herbs, olives, artichokes, and feta cheese. It's sure to be a hit around the campfire!

**Campfire Pesto Pasta with Cherry Tomatoes**

Ingredients:

- 8 ounces (about 225g) pasta (such as penne, fusilli, or rotini)
- 1/4 cup basil pesto (homemade or store-bought)
- 1 cup cherry tomatoes, halved
- 2 tablespoons olive oil
- 2 cloves garlic, minced
- Salt and black pepper, to taste
- Grated Parmesan cheese, for serving
- Fresh basil leaves, chopped, for garnish (optional)

Instructions:

1. Cook the pasta according to the package instructions until al dente. Drain and set aside.
2. Heat a large skillet or Dutch oven over medium heat, either on a campfire grate or a camp stove.
3. Add the olive oil to the skillet or Dutch oven and heat it until shimmering.
4. Add the minced garlic to the skillet and cook for about 1 minute, or until fragrant.
5. Add the halved cherry tomatoes to the skillet and cook for 2-3 minutes, or until they start to soften and release their juices.
6. Stir in the cooked pasta and basil pesto, tossing to coat the pasta evenly with the pesto sauce and tomatoes. Cook for another 1-2 minutes to heat through.
7. Season the Campfire Pesto Pasta with salt and black pepper, to taste.
8. Once heated through, remove the skillet or Dutch oven from the heat.
9. Serve the Campfire Pesto Pasta hot, garnished with grated Parmesan cheese and chopped fresh basil leaves, if desired.
10. Enjoy the delicious and flavorful Campfire Pesto Pasta with Cherry Tomatoes as a satisfying camping meal!

This Campfire Pesto Pasta with Cherry Tomatoes is quick and easy to make, and it's packed with the fresh flavors of basil pesto and juicy cherry tomatoes. It's sure to be a hit around the campfire!

**Dutch Oven Chicken and Dumplings**

Ingredients:

For the Chicken Stew:

- 2 tablespoons olive oil
- 1 onion, diced
- 2 carrots, diced
- 2 celery stalks, diced
- 2 cloves garlic, minced
- 1 teaspoon dried thyme
- 1 teaspoon dried rosemary
- 1 bay leaf
- Salt and black pepper, to taste
- 4 cups chicken broth
- 1 pound boneless, skinless chicken breasts or thighs, cut into bite-sized pieces
- 1 cup frozen peas

For the Dumplings:

- 1 cup all-purpose flour
- 1 1/2 teaspoons baking powder
- 1/2 teaspoon salt
- 1/2 cup milk
- 2 tablespoons unsalted butter, melted

Instructions:

1. Heat a Dutch oven over medium heat, either on a campfire grate or a camp stove.
2. Add the olive oil to the Dutch oven and heat it until shimmering.
3. Add the diced onion, carrots, and celery to the Dutch oven, and cook until the vegetables are softened, about 5-7 minutes.
4. Stir in the minced garlic, dried thyme, dried rosemary, bay leaf, salt, and black pepper, and cook for another minute until fragrant.
5. Pour the chicken broth into the Dutch oven, stirring to combine with the vegetables and spices.
6. Add the bite-sized pieces of chicken to the Dutch oven, stirring to submerge them in the broth.

7. Cover the Dutch oven with its lid and let the chicken stew simmer over medium-low heat for about 20-25 minutes, or until the chicken is cooked through and the vegetables are tender.
8. Meanwhile, prepare the dumplings. In a mixing bowl, whisk together the all-purpose flour, baking powder, and salt.
9. In a separate bowl, combine the milk and melted butter.
10. Pour the milk mixture into the flour mixture, stirring until just combined to form a thick batter.
11. Once the chicken stew is cooked, remove the bay leaf from the Dutch oven.
12. Drop spoonfuls of the dumpling batter onto the surface of the simmering chicken stew.
13. Cover the Dutch oven again with its lid and let the chicken stew simmer for another 15-20 minutes, or until the dumplings are cooked through and fluffy.
14. Stir in the frozen peas and cook for another 2-3 minutes until heated through.
15. Serve the Dutch Oven Chicken and Dumplings hot, and enjoy the comforting and hearty flavors!

This Dutch Oven Chicken and Dumplings recipe is sure to be a hit with everyone around the campfire.

It's easy to make and packed with delicious flavors, making it the perfect camping comfort food!

**Campfire Ratatouille Stuffed Mushrooms**

Ingredients:

- 8 large portobello mushrooms, stems removed and gills scraped out
- 1 small eggplant, diced
- 1 zucchini, diced
- 1 yellow squash, diced
- 1 red bell pepper, diced
- 1 onion, diced
- 2 cloves garlic, minced
- 2 tablespoons olive oil
- 1 teaspoon dried thyme
- 1 teaspoon dried oregano
- Salt and black pepper, to taste
- 1/4 cup grated Parmesan cheese
- Fresh basil leaves, chopped, for garnish (optional)

Instructions:

1. Prepare your campfire grill or a grill grate over medium heat.
2. In a large skillet, heat the olive oil over medium heat, either on a campfire grate or a camp stove.
3. Add the diced eggplant, zucchini, yellow squash, red bell pepper, onion, and minced garlic to the skillet.
4. Cook the vegetables, stirring occasionally, until they are softened and starting to brown, about 8-10 minutes.
5. Stir in the dried thyme and dried oregano, and season with salt and black pepper, to taste. Cook for another minute until the herbs are fragrant.
6. Remove the skillet from the heat and let the ratatouille mixture cool slightly.
7. Spoon the ratatouille mixture into the cavity of each portobello mushroom, dividing it evenly among the mushrooms.
8. Sprinkle grated Parmesan cheese over the top of each stuffed mushroom.
9. Place the stuffed mushrooms on the preheated grill grate over the campfire.
10. Cook the Campfire Ratatouille Stuffed Mushrooms for about 10-15 minutes, or until the mushrooms are tender and the cheese is melted and bubbly.
11. Once cooked, carefully remove the stuffed mushrooms from the grill using tongs or a spatula.
12. Garnish the stuffed mushrooms with chopped fresh basil leaves, if desired.
13. Serve the Campfire Ratatouille Stuffed Mushrooms hot, and enjoy their delicious and savory flavors!

These Campfire Ratatouille Stuffed Mushrooms are a delightful and satisfying dish that's perfect for camping. They're easy to make and packed with the rich flavors of ratatouille, making them a hit with everyone around the campfire!

**Grilled Halloumi and Vegetable Skewers**

Ingredients:

- 1 block halloumi cheese, cut into cubes
- 1 red bell pepper, cut into chunks
- 1 yellow bell pepper, cut into chunks
- 1 zucchini, sliced into rounds
- 1 red onion, cut into chunks
- Cherry tomatoes
- Olive oil, for brushing
- Salt and black pepper, to taste
- Fresh herbs (such as basil or parsley), chopped, for garnish (optional)
- Lemon wedges, for serving

Instructions:

1. If using wooden skewers, soak them in water for at least 30 minutes to prevent them from burning on the grill.
2. Preheat your campfire grill or a grill grate over medium heat.
3. Thread the halloumi cubes and prepared vegetables onto the skewers, alternating them as desired.
4. Brush the skewers with olive oil and season them with salt and black pepper to taste.
5. Place the skewers on the preheated grill grate over the campfire.
6. Grill the Halloumi and Vegetable Skewers for about 5-7 minutes on each side, or until the vegetables are tender and the halloumi is lightly charred.
7. Once cooked, carefully remove the skewers from the grill using tongs or a spatula.
8. Transfer the skewers to a serving platter and garnish with chopped fresh herbs, if desired.
9. Serve the Grilled Halloumi and Vegetable Skewers hot, accompanied by lemon wedges for squeezing over the skewers for extra flavor.
10. Enjoy these delicious and flavorful skewers as a satisfying camping meal or appetizer!

These Grilled Halloumi and Vegetable Skewers are sure to be a hit around the campfire. They're easy to make, packed with delicious flavors, and perfect for enjoying the great outdoors!

**Foil Packet Honey Garlic Chicken**

Ingredients:

- 4 boneless, skinless chicken breasts
- 1/4 cup honey
- 3 cloves garlic, minced
- 2 tablespoons soy sauce
- 1 tablespoon olive oil
- Salt and black pepper, to taste
- Optional: chopped green onions or sesame seeds for garnish

Instructions:

1. Preheat your campfire grill or a grill grate over medium heat.
2. Tear off four large sheets of heavy-duty aluminum foil, each large enough to fully wrap around one chicken breast with some extra space.
3. Place one chicken breast in the center of each piece of foil.
4. In a small bowl, whisk together the honey, minced garlic, soy sauce, and olive oil until well combined.
5. Drizzle the honey garlic sauce over each chicken breast, coating them evenly on all sides. Season the chicken with salt and black pepper, to taste.
6. Fold the sides of the foil over the chicken to create a packet, sealing it tightly to prevent any juices from leaking out during cooking.
7. Place the foil packets directly onto the preheated grill grate over the campfire.
8. Cook the Foil Packet Honey Garlic Chicken for about 15-20 minutes, flipping the packets halfway through cooking, or until the chicken is cooked through and reaches an internal temperature of 165°F (75°C).
9. Once cooked, carefully remove the foil packets from the grill using tongs or heatproof gloves.
10. Carefully open the foil packets, taking care to avoid the steam.
11. Transfer the cooked chicken breasts to a serving platter, and drizzle any remaining sauce from the foil packets over the top.
12. Optional: Garnish the Foil Packet Honey Garlic Chicken with chopped green onions or sesame seeds for extra flavor and presentation.
13. Serve the chicken hot, and enjoy the tender and flavorful honey garlic chicken!

This Foil Packet Honey Garlic Chicken is a simple and delicious camping meal that's sure to be a hit with everyone around the campfire. It's easy to make, packed with flavor, and perfect for enjoying the great outdoors!

**Campfire Stuffed Apples with Cinnamon**

Ingredients:

- 4 large apples (such as Granny Smith or Honeycrisp)
- 1/4 cup brown sugar
- 1/4 cup old-fashioned oats
- 2 tablespoons unsalted butter, softened
- 1 teaspoon ground cinnamon
- 1/4 teaspoon ground nutmeg
- 1/4 cup chopped nuts (such as pecans or walnuts), optional
- Vanilla ice cream or whipped cream, for serving (optional)

Instructions:

1. Preheat your campfire or charcoal grill to medium heat.
2. Core the apples, removing the seeds and creating a cavity in the center of each apple to hold the stuffing. You can use an apple corer or a paring knife to do this.
3. In a small bowl, combine the brown sugar, oats, softened butter, ground cinnamon, ground nutmeg, and chopped nuts (if using). Mix well until the ingredients are evenly incorporated.
4. Spoon the stuffing mixture into the cavities of the cored apples, dividing it evenly among them.
5. Wrap each stuffed apple individually in a double layer of heavy-duty aluminum foil, making sure to seal the foil tightly to prevent any juices from leaking out during cooking.
6. Place the foil-wrapped stuffed apples directly onto the preheated campfire or grill grate.
7. Cook the Campfire Stuffed Apples for about 20-25 minutes, turning them occasionally, or until the apples are tender and the filling is bubbling.
8. Once cooked, carefully remove the foil-wrapped apples from the campfire or grill using tongs or heatproof gloves.
9. Carefully unwrap the foil from each stuffed apple, taking care to avoid the steam.
10. Serve the Campfire Stuffed Apples hot, optionally topped with a scoop of vanilla ice cream or a dollop of whipped cream.
11. Enjoy the warm and comforting flavors of the Campfire Stuffed Apples with Cinnamon as a delicious camping dessert!

These Campfire Stuffed Apples with Cinnamon are a simple yet indulgent treat that's perfect for enjoying around the campfire. They're easy to make and packed with sweet, spiced goodness that's sure to satisfy your camping cravings!

**Dutch Oven Beef Stew**

Ingredients:

- 4 large apples (such as Granny Smith or Honeycrisp)
- 1/4 cup brown sugar
- 1/4 cup old-fashioned oats
- 2 tablespoons unsalted butter, softened
- 1 teaspoon ground cinnamon
- 1/4 teaspoon ground nutmeg
- 1/4 cup chopped nuts (such as pecans or walnuts), optional
- Vanilla ice cream or whipped cream, for serving (optional)

Instructions:

1. Preheat your campfire or charcoal grill to medium heat.
2. Core the apples, removing the seeds and creating a cavity in the center of each apple to hold the stuffing. You can use an apple corer or a paring knife to do this.
3. In a small bowl, combine the brown sugar, oats, softened butter, ground cinnamon, ground nutmeg, and chopped nuts (if using). Mix well until the ingredients are evenly incorporated.
4. Spoon the stuffing mixture into the cavities of the cored apples, dividing it evenly among them.
5. Wrap each stuffed apple individually in a double layer of heavy-duty aluminum foil, making sure to seal the foil tightly to prevent any juices from leaking out during cooking.
6. Place the foil-wrapped stuffed apples directly onto the preheated campfire or grill grate.
7. Cook the Campfire Stuffed Apples for about 20-25 minutes, turning them occasionally, or until the apples are tender and the filling is bubbling.
8. Once cooked, carefully remove the foil-wrapped apples from the campfire or grill using tongs or heatproof gloves.
9. Carefully unwrap the foil from each stuffed apple, taking care to avoid the steam.
10. Serve the Campfire Stuffed Apples hot, optionally topped with a scoop of vanilla ice cream or a dollop of whipped cream.
11. Enjoy the warm and comforting flavors of the Campfire Stuffed Apples with Cinnamon as a delicious camping dessert!

These Campfire Stuffed Apples with Cinnamon are a simple yet indulgent treat that's perfect for enjoying around the campfire. They're easy to make and packed with sweet, spiced goodness that's sure to satisfy your camping cravings!

**Dutch Oven Beef Stew**

Dutch Oven Beef Stew is a classic and hearty dish that's perfect for camping. Here's how to prepare it:

Ingredients:

- 2 pounds beef stew meat, cut into bite-sized pieces
- 2 tablespoons vegetable oil
- 1 onion, diced
- 2 cloves garlic, minced
- 4 carrots, peeled and sliced
- 4 potatoes, peeled and diced
- 2 celery stalks, sliced
- 4 cups beef broth
- 1 cup red wine (optional)
- 2 tablespoons tomato paste
- 2 bay leaves
- 1 teaspoon dried thyme
- Salt and black pepper, to taste
- 1/4 cup all-purpose flour (optional, for thickening)
- Chopped fresh parsley, for garnish (optional)

Instructions:

1. Heat a Dutch oven over medium heat, either on a campfire grate or a camp stove.
2. Add the vegetable oil to the Dutch oven and heat it until shimmering.
3. Add the beef stew meat to the Dutch oven in batches, searing it on all sides until browned. Remove the browned meat from the Dutch oven and set it aside.
4. Add the diced onion and minced garlic to the Dutch oven, and cook until softened and fragrant, about 3-4 minutes.
5. Return the browned beef stew meat to the Dutch oven.
6. Add the sliced carrots, diced potatoes, sliced celery, beef broth, red wine (if using), tomato paste, bay leaves, and dried thyme to the Dutch oven. Stir well to combine.
7. Season the beef stew with salt and black pepper, to taste.
8. If you prefer a thicker stew, you can sprinkle the flour over the stew and stir to combine. This will help thicken the sauce as it cooks.
9. Cover the Dutch oven with its lid and let the beef stew simmer over low heat for about 1.5 to 2 hours, or until the meat is tender and the vegetables are cooked through.
10. Once the beef stew is cooked, taste and adjust the seasoning if necessary.
11. Remove the bay leaves from the Dutch oven before serving.

12. Ladle the Dutch Oven Beef Stew into bowls, and garnish with chopped fresh parsley, if desired.
13. Serve the beef stew hot, and enjoy the comforting and hearty flavors!

This Dutch Oven Beef Stew is a comforting and satisfying meal that's perfect for camping. It's easy to make and packed with rich flavors that are sure to warm you up on chilly nights outdoors!

**Campfire Breakfast Burritos**

Ingredients:

- 6 large eggs
- 1 tablespoon butter or oil
- Salt and pepper, to taste
- 6 large flour tortillas
- 1 cup cooked breakfast meat (such as bacon, sausage, or ham), chopped
- 1 cup shredded cheese (such as cheddar or Monterey Jack)
- Optional fillings: diced bell peppers, onions, tomatoes, spinach, salsa, avocado, sour cream, etc.

Instructions:

1. Prepare your campfire grill or a camp stove over medium heat.
2. In a large skillet, melt the butter or heat the oil over medium heat, either on the campfire grill or camp stove.
3. Crack the eggs into a bowl, and season them with salt and pepper. Whisk the eggs until well beaten.
4. Pour the beaten eggs into the skillet, and cook, stirring occasionally, until they are scrambled and cooked through. Remove the skillet from the heat and set aside.
5. Warm the flour tortillas on the campfire grill or directly over the flames for a few seconds on each side until they are pliable and heated through. Be careful not to burn them.
6. Lay out the warmed tortillas on a clean surface.
7. Divide the scrambled eggs evenly among the tortillas, placing a portion of eggs in the center of each tortilla.
8. Top the scrambled eggs with cooked breakfast meat, shredded cheese, and any optional fillings you desire.
9. To fold the burritos, fold the sides of the tortilla over the filling, then fold the bottom edge up over the filling, and roll tightly to enclose the filling completely.
10. Repeat the process with the remaining tortillas and filling ingredients.
11. If desired, wrap each Campfire Breakfast Burrito individually in aluminum foil to keep them warm and make them easier to handle.
12. Place the wrapped burritos on the campfire grill or camp stove, and cook for a few minutes on each side until they are heated through and the cheese is melted.
13. Once heated through, remove the Campfire Breakfast Burritos from the grill or stove, and unwrap them from the foil if necessary.
14. Serve the breakfast burritos hot, and enjoy them with your favorite toppings such as salsa, avocado, sour cream, or hot sauce.

These Campfire Breakfast Burritos are a delicious and customizable meal that's perfect for fueling up before a day of outdoor adventures. They're easy to make, easy to eat on the go, and sure to satisfy your hunger while camping!

**Foil Packet Lemon Herb Tilapia**

Ingredients:

- 4 tilapia fillets
- 2 tablespoons olive oil
- 2 cloves garlic, minced
- 1 lemon, thinly sliced
- 2 tablespoons fresh lemon juice
- 2 tablespoons chopped fresh parsley
- 1 tablespoon chopped fresh dill
- Salt and black pepper, to taste
- Optional: sliced cherry tomatoes, sliced bell peppers, thinly sliced onions

Instructions:

1. Preheat your campfire grill or a grill grate over medium heat.
2. Tear off four large sheets of heavy-duty aluminum foil, each large enough to fully wrap around one tilapia fillet with some extra space.
3. Place one tilapia fillet in the center of each piece of foil.
4. In a small bowl, whisk together the olive oil, minced garlic, fresh lemon juice, chopped parsley, chopped dill, salt, and black pepper.
5. Drizzle the lemon herb mixture over each tilapia fillet, coating them evenly.
6. Place 2-3 slices of lemon on top of each tilapia fillet.
7. If desired, add any optional ingredients such as sliced cherry tomatoes, sliced bell peppers, or thinly sliced onions on top of the tilapia fillets.
8. Fold the sides of the foil over the tilapia to create a packet, sealing it tightly to prevent any juices from leaking out during cooking.
9. Place the foil packets directly onto the preheated grill grate over the campfire.
10. Cook the Foil Packet Lemon Herb Tilapia for about 10-12 minutes, or until the fish is cooked through and flakes easily with a fork.
11. Once cooked, carefully remove the foil packets from the grill using tongs or a spatula.
12. Carefully open the foil packets, taking care to avoid the steam.
13. Serve the Foil Packet Lemon Herb Tilapia hot, and enjoy the light and flavorful fish!

This Foil Packet Lemon Herb Tilapia is a simple and delicious camping meal that's quick to prepare and packed with fresh flavors. It's perfect for enjoying the great outdoors!

**Skillet Chicken Alfredo**

Ingredients:

- 8 ounces fettuccine or your favorite pasta
- 2 boneless, skinless chicken breasts, cut into bite-sized pieces
- 2 tablespoons olive oil
- 2 cloves garlic, minced
- 1 cup heavy cream
- 1 cup grated Parmesan cheese
- Salt and black pepper, to taste
- Optional: chopped fresh parsley or basil, for garnish

Instructions:

1. Cook the fettuccine according to the package instructions until al dente. Drain and set aside.
2. Heat a large skillet over medium heat, either on a campfire grate or a camp stove.
3. Add the olive oil to the skillet and heat it until shimmering.
4. Add the minced garlic to the skillet and cook for about 1 minute, or until fragrant.
5. Add the bite-sized pieces of chicken to the skillet, season with salt and black pepper, and cook until browned and cooked through, about 6-8 minutes.
6. Reduce the heat to medium-low and pour the heavy cream into the skillet, stirring to combine with the chicken and garlic.
7. Cook the chicken and cream mixture, stirring occasionally, until the sauce thickens slightly, about 3-5 minutes.
8. Stir in the grated Parmesan cheese until melted and smooth, creating a creamy Alfredo sauce.
9. Add the cooked fettuccine to the skillet, tossing to coat the pasta evenly with the sauce.
10. Cook for another 1-2 minutes, allowing the pasta to heat through and absorb some of the sauce.
11. Once heated through, remove the skillet from the heat.
12. Garnish the Skillet Chicken Alfredo with chopped fresh parsley or basil, if desired.
13. Serve the Skillet Chicken Alfredo hot, and enjoy the creamy and comforting flavors!

This Skillet Chicken Alfredo is a simple and delicious camping meal that's sure to satisfy your hunger after a day of outdoor adventures. It's easy to make and packed with creamy, cheesy goodness!

**Campfire Caprese Salad**

Ingredients:

- 4 large ripe tomatoes, sliced
- 8 ounces fresh mozzarella cheese, sliced
- Fresh basil leaves
- Balsamic glaze
- Extra virgin olive oil
- Salt and black pepper, to taste

Instructions:

1. Preheat your campfire grill or a grill grate over medium heat.
2. Arrange the tomato slices and fresh mozzarella slices alternately on a serving platter or individual plates.
3. Place a fresh basil leaf on top of each tomato and mozzarella slice.
4. Drizzle balsamic glaze and extra virgin olive oil over the tomato and mozzarella slices.
5. Season the Campfire Caprese Salad with salt and black pepper, to taste.
6. Once the campfire grill is preheated, place the serving platter or plates on the grill grate.
7. Grill the Caprese Salad for 1-2 minutes, just until the mozzarella begins to soften slightly and the flavors meld together. Be careful not to overcook.
8. Once grilled, carefully remove the serving platter or plates from the grill using tongs or a spatula.
9. Serve the Campfire Caprese Salad immediately, while still warm from the grill.
10. Enjoy the fresh and vibrant flavors of the Campfire Caprese Salad as a delicious side dish or appetizer while camping!

This Campfire Caprese Salad is a simple yet elegant dish that's perfect for enjoying the great outdoors. It's easy to make and bursting with the flavors of ripe tomatoes, creamy mozzarella, and fragrant basil, all enhanced by the tangy balsamic glaze and extra virgin olive oil.

**Dutch Oven Vegetarian Chili**

Ingredients:

- 2 tablespoons olive oil
- 1 onion, diced
- 2 cloves garlic, minced
- 1 bell pepper, diced
- 1 zucchini, diced
- 1 carrot, diced
- 1 can (15 ounces) black beans, drained and rinsed
- 1 can (15 ounces) kidney beans, drained and rinsed
- 1 can (15 ounces) diced tomatoes
- 1 cup corn kernels (fresh, frozen, or canned)
- 2 cups vegetable broth
- 2 tablespoons chili powder
- 1 teaspoon ground cumin
- 1 teaspoon smoked paprika
- Salt and black pepper, to taste
- Optional toppings: shredded cheese, diced avocado, sour cream, chopped cilantro, lime wedges, etc.

Instructions:

1. Heat a Dutch oven over medium heat, either on a campfire grate or a camp stove.
2. Add the olive oil to the Dutch oven and heat it until shimmering.
3. Add the diced onion, minced garlic, diced bell pepper, diced zucchini, and diced carrot to the Dutch oven. Cook, stirring occasionally, until the vegetables are softened, about 5-7 minutes.
4. Add the drained and rinsed black beans, kidney beans, diced tomatoes, corn kernels, vegetable broth, chili powder, ground cumin, smoked paprika, salt, and black pepper to the Dutch oven. Stir well to combine.
5. Bring the chili to a simmer, then reduce the heat to low.
6. Cover the Dutch oven with its lid and let the chili simmer for about 30-40 minutes, stirring occasionally, to allow the flavors to meld together and the vegetables to become tender.
7. Once the chili is cooked and the vegetables are tender, taste and adjust the seasoning if necessary.
8. Serve the Dutch Oven Vegetarian Chili hot, ladled into bowls and topped with your favorite toppings such as shredded cheese, diced avocado, sour cream, chopped cilantro, or a squeeze of lime juice.
9. Enjoy the hearty and flavorful Dutch Oven Vegetarian Chili as a satisfying camping meal!

This Dutch Oven Vegetarian Chili is packed with wholesome ingredients and bold flavors, making it a delicious and comforting dish for enjoying around the campfire. It's easy to make and perfect for fueling up during outdoor adventures!

**Campfire Sausage and Potato Foil Packets**

Ingredients:

- 1 pound smoked sausage, sliced into rounds
- 4 medium potatoes, thinly sliced
- 1 onion, thinly sliced
- 2 cloves garlic, minced
- 2 tablespoons olive oil
- 1 teaspoon paprika
- 1 teaspoon dried thyme
- Salt and black pepper, to taste
- Optional: chopped fresh parsley or green onions, for garnish

Instructions:

1. Preheat your campfire grill or a grill grate over medium heat.
2. Tear off four large sheets of heavy-duty aluminum foil, each large enough to fully wrap around one foil packet with some extra space.
3. In a large bowl, combine the sliced smoked sausage, thinly sliced potatoes, thinly sliced onion, minced garlic, olive oil, paprika, dried thyme, salt, and black pepper. Toss until the ingredients are well coated.
4. Divide the sausage and potato mixture evenly among the four sheets of aluminum foil, placing it in the center of each sheet.
5. Fold the sides of the foil over the sausage and potato mixture to create a packet, sealing it tightly to prevent any juices from leaking out during cooking.
6. Place the foil packets directly onto the preheated grill grate over the campfire.
7. Cook the Campfire Sausage and Potato Foil Packets for about 20-25 minutes, flipping them halfway through cooking, or until the potatoes are tender and the sausage is heated through.
8. Once cooked, carefully remove the foil packets from the grill using tongs or a spatula.
9. Carefully open the foil packets, taking care to avoid the steam.
10. If desired, garnish the Campfire Sausage and Potato Foil Packets with chopped fresh parsley or green onions for a pop of color and freshness.
11. Serve the foil packets hot, and enjoy the hearty and flavorful combination of sausage and potatoes!

These Campfire Sausage and Potato Foil Packets are a simple and satisfying camping meal that's easy to make and packed with delicious flavors. They're perfect for enjoying around the campfire after a day of outdoor adventures!

www.ingramcontent.com/pod-product-compliance
Lightning Source LLC
LaVergne TN
LVHW061946070526
838199LV00060B/4003